Diet recommendations during TCM - Lung - Wind-cold affects the Lung

Please check these recommendations always with a nutrition consultant, therapist, doctor or dietician. The recipes and the list of ingredients are supporting the conventional medical therapy. The calorie disclosures of fresh ingredients (fruit and vegetables) vary according to quality and time of harvest. The contents were checked by a dietician and a nutrition consultant for the Traditional Chinese Medicine (TCM).

Author:
©2020 Josef Miligui
www.ebns.at

AF220177

Source:
The lists are created from the EBNS database for nutritional counseling. The database is used by dietitians, therapists and doctors for advising the patient / client.

Literature:
The specialist literature and the training documents of the German and Austrian dietary and traditional Chinese medicine serve as a knowledge base. We have used the documents as a basis of knowledge, adapted it to our experience and completed them.
http://nutribook.info/

Production and publishing:
BoD – Books on Demand, Norderstedt
ISBN: 9783752833157

Diet recommendations for TCM - Lung - Wind-cold affects the Lung

1 Treatment strategy

Drain (open surface and expel cold), strengthen lungs Qi, strengthen middle. Hot YES (except bitter), warm and neutral YES (except sour), refreshing and cold NO

2 Avoid

Sour foods, tropical fruits, unripe fruits, very sweet food, dairy products, power soups, chicken meat, eggs, peppermint, lime blossom, elderflower.

3 Breakfast

kkal. per serving

Compote from cherries	31
Lettuce with vinegar dressing	67
Pine nuts porridge	235
Polenta with peach	197
Recipe against cold by wind-cold evil 1	67
Rice porridge with shallots	177
Tea from anise	2
Tea from cinnamon sticks	2
Tea from lime blossom	0
Tea from marjoram	0,5
Tender fennel vegetables - also for babies from 6th month	70
Warming porridge	35

4   Snack

5   Lunch

6   Afternoon

7   Dinner

8 Any time

9 Recipes

(rec.) = You can use more.
(little) = You should use less than specified
(omit) = omit.

9.1 Compote from cherries

Moisturizes liver and kidney, forces middle, reduces blood congestion, reduces internal heat, warms the stomach and spleen, promotes blood circulation and conduction flow, relieves cold-sickness and pain.
Cooking time approx. 10 min
Calories p. portion: 32
2 portions

Quantity of ingredients

Cherry 1/4 lbs - 4oz / 100g. (yes) - warm - sweet, sour .... earth
Water 1 1/2 cups / 240g. (yes) - cool - salty.. earth
Cinnamon ground 1 pinch / 0,2g. (rec.) - hot - acrid, sweet .... *

Cooking instructions:

Cook the cherries in the water until soft. Sprinkle with a little cinnamon.

9.2   Fennel with roasted walnuts

Regulates Qi, warms the inside, lowers coldness, strengthens the stomach, relieves constipation, strengthens kidneys and spleen Yang, dissolves mucus, reduces wind, reduce cold evil, soften knots, strengthens stomach Qi.
Cooking time approx. 20 min
Calories p. portion: 342
4 portions
Allergens: HO

Quantity of ingredients
Fennel 4 pieces / 800g. (rec.) - warm - sweet, little acrid .... earth
Nutmeg 1 pinch / 1g. (rec.) - warm - acrid .... metal
Ginger fresh 1/2 teaspoon / 1g. (rec.) - warm - acrid .... metal
Salt 1 pinch / 1g. (little) - cold - salty .... water
White wine 1/2 cup / 125g. (yes) - cool - sweet, bitter, acrid .... wood
Olive oil 2 table spoons / 40g. () - cool - sweet .... earth
Walnuts 2 table spoons / 35g. (yes) - warm - sweet .... earth
Water 1 1/2 cups / 220g. (yes) - cool - salty .... earth
Corn Grease (Polenta) 1 cup / 120g. (yes) - neutral - sweet .... earth
Salt 1 pinch / 1g. (little) - cold - salty .... water

Cooking instructions:
Heat very little water in a pot; Fry the fennel in strips. Add Nutmeg, a little grated ginger, add salt, a dash of white wine, rose paprika.
Simmer until the vegetables are cooked, but still crisp; stir in a little olive oil; sprinkle with roasted walnuts.

Stir the polenta into a pot of hot water, stirring constantly, until the polenta has the desired consistency. Salt.
Pull the polenta off the fire and let it swell for about 10 minutes.

9.3   Ginger garlic drink

Dissolves stagnation, directs upwards, gets Qi moving, reduces cold-evil, directs upwards, forces Qi and spleen, reduces cold-evil and inner wind.
Cooking time approx. 30 min
Calories p. portion: 34
2 portions

Quantity of ingredients

Ginger fresh 1/2 oz / 15g. (rec.) - warm - acrid .... metal
Garlic 1/2 oz / 15g. (rec.) - hot - acrid.. metal
Sugar brown 1 table spoon / 10g. () - warm - sweet .... earth
Water 2 cup / 500g. (yes) - cool - salty... earth

Cooking instructions:
Simmer all ingredients in a pot for 1/2 hour, then strain.

9.4 Lettuce with vinegar dressing

Cools in internal heat, dries out, regulates Qi, warms spleen and kidney,
dissolves stagnation, moisturizes, laxative, antiparasitic, nourishes Yin,
moisturizes, relaxes, builds up Qi, spreads. brings blood into motion,
preserves the fluids, contracts.
Cooking time approx. 10 min
Calories p. portion: 68
2 portions
Allergens: O

Quantity of ingredients

Lettuce 1 piece / 200g. (yes) - cool - sweet. bitter... fire
Vinegar (Apple vinegar) 1 table spoon / 10g. (yes) - warm - sour, bitter ....wood
Water 1 table spoon / 10g. (yes) - cool - sa ty... earth
Rapeseed oil 1 table spoon / 10g. (yes) - neutral - sweet .... earth
Onion (spring onion) 1 piece / 20g. (rec.) - warm - acrid .... metal
Salt 1 pinch / 0,5g. (little) - cold - salty .... water
Pepper (ground) 1 pinch / 0,1g. () - warm - acrid .... metal
Chives 1 table spoon / 5g. (rec.) - warm - acrid .... metal

Cooking instructions:
Clean lettuce, wash and drain. Add the ingredients to the marinade in
an extra container. Salad with marinade just
before consumption. Just before, sprinkle with chives.

9.5 Oatmeal soup with spring onion and carrots

Strengthens spleen and liver, regulates Qi flow, moisturizes, relaxes,
builds up Qi, spreads, moisturizes intestines, regulates Qi, warms
spleen and kidney, dissolves stagnation, directs upwards.
Cooking time approx. 30 min
Calories p. portion: 135
3 portions
Allergens: AG

Quantity of ingredients

Oat 6 table spoons / 48g. (yes) - warm - sweet... metal
Carrot 2 pieces / 200g. (rec.) - neutral - sweet.. earth
Butter organic 1 table spoon / 15g. (yes) - neutral - sweet........................ earth
Nutmeg 1 pinch / 1g. (rec.) - warm - acrid.. metal
Lovage 1 stem / 15g. (rec.) - warm - acrid, bitter .... metal
Onion (spring onion) 2 pieces / 40g. (rec.) - warm - acrid .... metal
Water 2 cup / 480g. (yes) - cool - salty.. earth

Cooking instructions:
Roast the oats in butter, add salt and spices, pour in water and heat till it boils. After 10 min. add the grated carrots and lovage, cook for 10 minutes. Finely add chopped onion.

9.6   Pine nuts porridge

Build up organs, feeds muscles, moisturizes, relaxes, builds up Qi, spreads.
Cooking time approx. 5 min
Calories p. portion: 235
1 portions

Quantity of ingredients
Pine nuts 2 table spoons / 35g. (yes) - neutral - sweet .... earth

Cooking instructions:
Available in good health food stores.

9.7   Polenta with peach

Strengthens blood and fluids, brings blood into motion, builds up Qi, spreads, strengthens stomach Qi, diuretic, moisturizes, relaxes, builds up Qi, spreads, warms the stomach and spleen, promotes blood circulation and conduction flow, relieves cold-sickness.
Cooking time approx. 20 min
Calories p. portion: 197
3 portions

Quantity of ingredients

Water 1 1/2 cups / 240g. (yes) - cool - salty... earth
Corn Grease (Polenta) 1 cup / 120g. (yes) - neutral - sweet...................... earth
Peaches 2-3 pieces / 400g. (yes) - warm - sour, sweet .... earth
Vanilla pod 1 pinch / 1g. () - neutral - sweet... *
Chili (pod or ground) 1 pinch / 0,1g. (rec.) - hot - acrid .... metal
Cinnamon ground 1 pinch / 1g. (rec.) - hot - acrid, sweet .... *

Cooking instructions:

Pour the polenta into a pan of hot water with constant stirring until the
polenta has the desired consistency. Pull the polenta from the fire and
let it soak for 10 minutes.

Wash fresh peaches and cut into quarters. Pour into the finished
polenta the peaches, add the vanilla and add Chili to taste, stir and let it
go for 3 minutes.

Winter varieties: Pickled fruit, pear, apples

9.8   Radish with spring onions and carrots

Nutritious, moisturizing and dynamizing, moves Qi and blood, dissolves
stagnation, directs upwards, strengthens stomach Qi, diuretic,
moisturizes, relaxes, builds up Qi, spreads. regulates Qi, warms spleen
and kidney.
Cooking time approx. 30 min
Calories p. portion: 246
2 portions
Allergens: EG

Quantity of ingredients

Carrot 2 pieces / 200g. (rec.) - neutral - sweet.. earth
Radish black 1/2 piece / 100g. (yes) - neutral - acrid .... metal
Ginger powder 1 knife tip / 0,2g. (rec.) - hot - acrid .... metal
Onion (spring onion) 1 piece / 20g. (rec.) - warm - acrid........................... metal
Salt 1 pinch / 0,5g. (little) - cold - salty .... water
Soy sauce 1 dash / 2g. () - cold - salty .... water
Lemon juice 2 table spoons / 16g. () - cold - sour ....wood
Curcuma 1 pinch / 0,2g. (yes) - warm - bitter.. *
Pepper powder (hot) 1 pinch / 0,2g. () - warm - bitter .... fire
Butter organic 1 teaspoon / 3g. (yes) - neutral - sweet .... earth
Water 1 cup / 250g. (yes) - cool - salty... earth
Corn Grease (Polenta) 1 cup / 100g. (yes) - neutral - sweet...................... earth
Salt 1 pinch / 0,5g. (little) - cold - salty .... water

Cooking instructions:
Cook finely chopped carrots, black or white finely chopped radish, a
pinch of grated ginger. Steam for 10 minutes, then strain.
In the meantime, stir in chopped spring onions, salt, soy sauce, a little
lemon juice, a pinch of turmeric or rose paprika and a piece of butter.

Garnish:
Stir the polenta into a pot of hot water, stirring constantly, until the
polenta has the desired texture. Pull the polenta off the fire and let it
swell for about 10 minutes.

9.9   Recipe against cold by wind-cold evil 1

Forces Qi and spleen, reduces cold-evil and inner wind, moisturizes,
relaxes, builds up Qi, spreads, directs
upwards, gets Qi moving.
Cooking time approx. 10 min
Calories p. portion: 67
1 portions

Quantity of ingredients
Ginger fresh 1/2 oz / 10g. (rec.) - warm - acrid .... metal
Sugar brown 1/2 oz / 15g. () - warm - sweet .... earth
Onion (spring onion) 1/4 piece / 7g. (rec.) - warm - acrid .... metal
Water 1/2 cup / 125g. (yes) - cool - salty .... earth

Cooking instructions:
Boil ginger and just the white parts of the spring onions together with
125 ml (about 1/2 cup) of water. When the water boils, add brown sugar
and stir.

Application: drink, go to bed after drinking, cover warm and sweat.

Frequency and duration of use
1-2 times a day, only in the first 24 hours.

9.10 Rice porridge with shallots

Warms the stomach and spleen, harmonizes the intestine, forces Qi, reduces moisture, regulates Qi, warms
spleen and kidney, dissolves stagnation, directs upwards.
Cooking time approx. 25 min
Calories p. portion: 177
2 portions

Quantity of ingredients
Rice variety any 1 cup / 100g. (yes) - warm - sweet .... metal
Water 4 cups / 400g. (yes) - cool - salty .... earth
Onion (spring onion) 2 table spoons / 12g. (rec.) - warm - acrid .... metal

Cooking instructions:
Boil the rice with the water until a porridge is formed. Finely chop onion and keep for 5 min. to let go.

9.11 Rice soup with grated carrots and fresh herbs

Strengthens spleen and liver, regulates Qi flow, moisturizes, relaxes, builds up Qi, spreads, forces kidney and
bladder.
Cooking time approx. 5 min
Calories p. portion: 131
4 portions
Allergens: EG

Quantity of ingredients
Rice wild (nature rice) 1 cup / 100g. (yes) - neutral - sweet, bitter .... metal
Water 6 cups / 700g. (yes) - cool - salty .... earth
Carrot 1 piece / 100g. (rec.) - neutral - sweet... earth
Soy sauce 1 dash / 2g. () - cold - salty .... water
Butter organic 1 teaspoon / 3g. (yes) - neutral - sweet .... earth
Ground 1 pinch / 0,3g. (yes) - warm - acrid .... metal
Curcuma 1 pinch / 0,2g. (yes) - warm - bitter ....*

Cooking instructions:
In a portion of rice congee according to basic recipe, softly cook a grated carrot, add butter and soy sauce.
Sprinkle with fresh herbs.
Spices and herbs: black cumin, turmeric, cardamom, parsley, sage, thyme, basil, rosemary.
Winter: parsnip, celery, onion, leek, pumpkin
Summer: tomatoes, zucchini, spring onion, radishes, arugula.

9.12 Sliced lamb with rosemary potatoes

Strengthens spleen and kidney Yang and stomach Qi, relieves weakness, heats middle and lower heater, forces
 Qi, relieves inflammation, moisturizes, relaxes, builds up Qi, spreads.
Cooking time approx. 1 hour
Calories p. portion: 461
4 portions
Allergens: LO

Quantity of ingredients

Lamb meat 7/8 lbs - 1 lbs / 500g. (rec.) - warm - sweet .... fire
Olive oil 2 table spoons / 20g. () - cool - sweet .... earth
Onion white 1 piece / 50g. (rec.) - warm - acrid .... metal
Garlic 1 clove / 2g. (rec.) - hot - acrid .... metal
Nutmeg 1 pinch / 0,2g. (rec.) - warm - acrid .... metal
Carrot 3 pieces / 150g. (rec.) - neutral - sweet .... earth
Celery root 1/4 tuber / 120g. (yes) - cool - sweet .... earth
Rosemary 1 Twig / 3g. (yes) - warm - bitter .... fire
Savory 1 teaspoon / 2g. () - warm - bitter .... water
Parsley 1 table spoon / 8g. (yes) - warm - bitter..wood
Pepper powder (hot) 1 pinch / 2g. () - warm - bitter .... fire
Red wine 1/2 cup / 125g. (yes) - warm - bitter .... fire
Lemon juice 1/2 piece / 15g. () - cold - sour ....wood
Cranberry 1 table spoon / 10g. () - cool - sour ....wood
Potato 6 pieces / 400g. (yes) - neutral - sweet .... earth

Cooking instructions:

Cut the lamb into strips, cut the carrots and celery into small cubes.

Heat the olive oil in a pan, fry the lamb in it, add the cut onions and garlic, salt with herbal salt, a little water, parsley, deglaze with red wine, season with paprika and small cut rosemary, mugwort, savory, carrots and celery, turn the heat back on small Simmer for about 35 minutes. Season with pepper and nutmeg, if necessary still salt, add a little lemon juice, season with paprika, cranberries.

Cut the potatoes in half, the length of, spread a little olive oil on the cut surface, salt, sprinkle 2-3 rosemary needles on each half potato, place the potatoes on the baking sheet and bake in a preheated oven for approx. 25 minutes at 190°C/374°F.

9.13 Spring vegetables - also for babies from the 8th month

Cools heat, diuretic, cools blood, reduces mucus, moisturizes, relaxes, builds Qi, distributes, strengthen the middle, nourishes lung Yin, produces humors.
Cooking time approx. 1 1/2 hour
Calories p. portion: 64
8 portions
Allergens: G

Quantity of ingredients
Carrot 1,1 lbs / 500g. (rec.) - neutral - sweet.. earth
Kohlrabi 1,1 lbs / 500g. (rec.) - neutral - acrid, sweet................................. earth
Butter organic 2 table spoons / 20g. (yes) - neutral - sweet........................ earth
Water 1/2 cup / 125g. (yes) - cool - salty.. earth

Cooking instructions:
Wash the vegetables thoroughly. Clean and peel carrots and turnip cabbage. From the turnip cabbage, finely chop some delicate leaves and set aside. Rasp the carrots and the turnip cabbage. Melt the butter, add the water and the vegetables and cook over medium heat for about 30 minutes. Stir occasionally. Spread the vegetables and cooked water to about 8 deep-frozen bags to a100-150 g (depending on the age of the child). Close the bags, allow them to cool down and freeze them for max 3 months.
If necessary, thaw, boil and mix with 80g of boiled potatoes and an egg. (The recipe can easily be varied if you want to use cauliflower, peas or zucchini)

9.14 Tea from anise

Warms the middle, forces stomach and spleen, warms stomach, reduces cold-evil, harmonizes stomach-Qi,
warms kidney.
Cooking time approx. 15 min
Calories p. portion: 3
4 portions

Quantity of ingredients
Anise (Common Fennel) 1 teaspoon / 3g. (rec.) - warm - acrid .... earth
Water 2 cup / 500g. (yes) - cool - salty.................... .... earth

Cooking instructions:
Heat the water till it boils and put it aside. Add anise.
10 min. to let go.
Pour through a tea strainer. Sweet to taste with honey.

In order to achieve a salutary effect, you should drink 2 cups of anise tea per day.

9.15 Tea from cinnamon sticks

Warms the stomach and spleen, promotes blood circulation and conduction flow, relieves cold-sickness and pain.
Cooking time approx. 15 min
Calories p. portion: 2
1 portions

Quantity of ingredients
Cinnamon sticks 1/4 piece / 1g. (rec.) - hot - acrid, sweet ....*
Water 1 cup / 125g. (yes) - cool - salty... earth

Cooking instructions:
A quarter of a cinnamon stick for a cup of tea. Start cold and bring to the boil. Let it sit for 15 minutes, then strain.
This tea is unsweetened and swallowed, slowly drunk. The amount is enough for one day.

9.16 Tea from coriander

Sudorific, reduces wind.
Cooking time approx. 10 min
Calories p. portion: 2
4 portions

Quantity of ingredients
Coriander 1 teaspoon / 3g. (rec.) - warm - acrid .... metal
Water 2 cup / 500g. (yes) - cool - salty... earth

Cooking instructions:
Heat the water till it boils and put it aside. Add coriander and 10 min. to let go. Sweet to taste with honey. Strain when pouring.

9.17 Tea from marjoram

Dissolves stagnation, directs upwards.
Cooking time approx. 10 min
Calories p. portion: 0
4 portions

Quantity of ingredients
Marjoram 2 teaspoons / 6g. (rec.) - warm - bitter .... metal
Water 2 cup / 500g. (yes) - cool - salty..................... .... earth

Cooking instructions:
Heat the water till it boils and put it aside. Add marjoram and 10 min. to let go. Sweet to taste with honey. Strain when pouring.

9.18 Tea from peppermint with white sugar

Cools heat, distributes mucus, derives wind-cold and wind-heat, brings the stomach Qi in motion, solves congestion, forces Qi, moisturizes lungs.
Cooking time approx. 15 min
Calories p. portion: 8
2 portions

Quantity of ingredients
Peppermint 1 table spoon / 7g. (little) - cool - acrid, bitter......................... metal
Water 2 cup / 500g. (yes) - cool - salty.. earth
Sugar candy white 1 teaspoon / 3g. () - neutral - sweet............................. earth

Cooking instructions:
Heat the water till it boils and put it aside. Add peppermint and 10 min. to let go. Strain. Sweet to taste with honey.

9.19 Tender fennel vegetables - also for babies from 6th month

Regulates Qi, warms the inside, lowers cold, forces stomach, relieves constipation, forces Yang, dissolves mucus, reduces wind, spreads.
Cooking time approx. 25 min
Calories p. portion: 70
2 portions
Allergens: G

Quantity of ingredients

Potato 1 piece / 50g. (yes) - neutral - sweet...earth
Fennel 1/4 lbs - 4oz / 100g. (rec.) - warm - sweet, little acrid.....................earth
Water 2 table spoons / 20g. (yes) - cool - salty ....earth
Butter organic 1 table spoon / 10g. (yes) - neutral - sweet..........................earth

Cooking instructions:

Wash the potato and peel with a peeler. Cut into cubes of about 2 cm.
Wash the fennel, remove stained, dark spots and cut the tuber. Heat till
it boils with 2 tablespoons of water in a small saucepan. Cook on low
heat for about 15 minutes. Fish out the caraway seeds. Puree the
vegetables with the blender and stir in the butter.
Fennel and caraway soothe the stomach and prevent bloating. In
addition, fennel contains a lot of vitamin C and folic acid. An ideal meal
for sick children.

9.20 Thick pea soup

Nourishes Qi, diuretic, harmonizes Qi (especially in the Middle and
Lower), strengthens the kidney and the defense Qi, discards moisture.
Cooking time approx. 2-3 hours
Calories p. portion: 123
3 portions
Allergens: AN

Quantity of ingredients

Peas, green 3/8 lbs - 6oz / 150g. (yes) - neutral - sweet............................ water
Water 2 1/4 cups / 550g. (yes) - cool - salty ....earth
Sesame oil 1 table spoon / 20g. () - cool - sweet ....earth
Onion white 1/2 piece / 25g. (rec.) - warm - acrid .... metal
Ginger fresh 1/2 teaspoon / 1g. (rec.) - warm - acrid .... metal
Ground 1/2 teaspoon / 1g. (yes) - warm - acrid...metal
Oat meal 1 table spoon / 15g. (yes) - warm - sweet................................... metal
Salt 1 pinch / 1g. (little) - cold - salty .... water
Parsley 1 stem / 2g. (yes) - warm - bitter ....wood

Cooking instructions:

Soak dried peas before cooking. Sauté sesame oil, onion, a little
oatmeal, ginger and cumin in a hot pot; add the peas and simmer for 2-
3 hours; add salt at the end and pruée with a blender; garnish with
parsley.

9.21 Warming porridge

Forces Qi and defensive power.
Cooking time approx. 10 min
Calories p. portion: 357
1 portions
Allergens: AHO

Quantity of ingredients
Oat flakes (whole grain) 6 table spoons / 60g. (rec.) - warm - sweet .... metal
Fig dried 3 pieces / 15g. (yes) - warm - sweet .... earth
Star anise 1 piece / 1g. (rec.) - warm - acrid .... *
Ginger fresh 1 pinch / 0,5g. (rec.) - warm - acrid...................................... metal
Water 1 cup / 120g. (yes) - cool - salty... earth
Maple syrup 1 table spoon / 10g. () - cool - sweet .... earth
Walnuts 1 table spoon (chopped) / 8g. (yes) - warm - sweet .... earth

Cooking instructions:
Soak the dried fruit. Roast Oatmeal dry. Add dried ginger, star anise or cinnamon, a little grated ginger and boil everything with water to a mash. With maple syrup sweet. Whip grated walnuts and sprinkle before serving.

Effect: Suitable for the cold season.
Caution: Fresh ginger does not drink over a long period of time.

10 Effects of food

10.1 Use ingredients: recommendable

Anise (Common Fennel)
Carrot
Carrot (Early Carrot)
Carrot juice without sugar
Chili (pod or ground)
Chives
Cinnamon ground
Cinnamon sticks
Clove
Coriander
Cumin (Caraway seed)
Curry
Deer meat
Dill
Fennel
Garlic

Ginger fresh
Ginger powder
Kohlrabi
Lamb meat
Leek
Lime b ossom tea
Lovage
Marjoram
Mustard seeds
Mutton
Nutmeg
Oat flakes (whole grain)
Oat fusion (baby food)
Onion (spring onion)
Onion read
Onion white

Pepper Cayenne
Pepper white (ground)
Peppercorns
Pheasant
Rabbit
Rabbit liver

Rabbit meat
Sour milk cheese 20%
Star anise
Turmeric (yellow root)
Wild boar meat

10.2 Use ingredients: yes

Almond marzipan
Almond milk
Almond puree
Apricot
Apricots
Basil
Basil (fresh)
Bean oil
Black tea
Boletus mushroom
Boxhorn clover seeds
Broad beans (thick beans)
Brussels sprouts
Butter organic
Celery root
Cereal coffee
Chanterelle
Cherry
Cherry juice
Chestnuts
Cocoa
Coconut flakes
Coconut grated
Coconut milk
Coffee
Corn Grease (Polenta)
Cress
Curcuma
Dates dried
Deer meat
Eel
Endive salad
Fig
Fig dried
French beans
Goat
Goat and sheep's milk
Goat cheese
Gourd
Grape juice red
Grape juice white
Green spelt
Ground
Ground caraway
Hawthorn

Hazelnuts
Herbs various
Hyssop
Iceberg lettuce
Juniper berry
Kumquats
Lentils black
Lentils red
Lettuce
Lobster
Longane
Malt
Morel (black, dried)
Morel, dried
Oat
Oat flour
Oat meal
Octopus
Okra
Olives
Onion (shallot)
Oregano dried
Oyster mushroom
Papaya
Parsley
Peaches
Peaches (canned)
Peanut oil
Peanuts
Peas
Peas, green
Peppers
Peppers (rose peppers)
Pigeon
Pine nuts
Pistachios
Pomegranate
Poppy
Pork heart
Pork knuckle
Pork liver
Pork stomach
Potato
Pumpkin
Pumpkin seed oil

Pumpkin seeds
Quail
Quail egg
Quinoa
Radish black
Raisins
Rapeseed oil
Red cabbage
Red wine
Rice (whole grain)
Rice black
Rice flour
Rice long grain rice
Rice malt
Rice noodles
Rice red
Rice round grain
Rice sweet
Rice variety any
Rice wild (nature rice)
Rose hip tea
Rosemary
Rye

Rye flour
Saffron
Sago (cereals)
Sake
Shiitake, dried
Shrimp
Soybean oil
Soybeans, black
Soybeans, yellow
Spiny lobsters
Sunflower seeds
Sweet potato
Thyme
Umeboshi plums (Japanese apricots)
Vanilla
Vanilla powder
Vinegar (Apple vinegar)
Walnuts
Water
Water hot
White beans
White wine

10.3 Use ingredients: little

Bitter melon
Breadcrumbs (wheat bread, bread roll)
Multi-grain bread (gray bread)
Peppermint

Rice Basmati
Salt
Soy Tofu
White bread (wheat bread)

10.4 Do not use contra-acting foods

Adzuki beans
Agar agar (kelp)
Amaranth
Anchovy / Sardine
Apple (sour)
Apple (sweet)
Apple juice (natural cloudy)
Arrowroot
Artichoke
Asparagus (green or white)
Aubergine
Avocado
Balm
Bamboo shoots
Banana
Banana (cooking banana)
Barley
Basic recipe for a beef soup (warming)
Basic recipe for a chicken soup
Basic recipe for a duck soup
Basic recipe for a fish soup

Basic recipe for a rice soup (Congee)
Basic recipe for a vegetable soup
(nutritious)
Beef fillet
Beef liver
Beef meat
Beef meat (calf)
Beef meatbones
Beef stomach
Beer (Pils)
Beer (Top-fermented German dark
beer)
Blackberry´s
Black-eyed peas
Blueberry
Blueberry juice
Broccoli
Buckwheat
Bulgur (cereals)
Burdock root tea
Buttermilk

Calamari
Cantaloupe
Carambola (Star fruit)
Carp
Cashews
Cauliflower
Caviar
Celery sticks
Champignon
Chard
Chicken egg
Chicken heart
Chicken liver
Chicken meat
Chicken stomach
Chicken yolk
Chickpeas
Chicory
Chinese cabbage
Chlorella (fresh water)
Clementines
Cod
Coix (seeds) YiYi Ren
Couscous
Cow's milk (1.5% fat)
Cow's milk (whole milk 3.5% fat)
Crab
Cranberry
Cranberry juice
Cream, sweet 30%
Crucian
Cucumber
Curd cheese 20%
Curd cheese 40%
Currant (black)
Currant (red)
Currant (white)
Dandelion (young plants)
Dandelionroots tea
Duck (heart)
Duck (slaughtered)
Elderberry blossom tee
Fennel tea
Feta chees
Fish pieces mixed (fresh water)
Fresh cheese
Goose
Goose egg
Goose parts
Gooseberry
Grapefruit (Pomelo)
Grapefruit juice
Grapes red
Grapes white

Grass carp
Green tea
Herring
Honey
Kefir
Kiwi
Kombu seaweed (Saccharina japonica)
Lamb's lettuce
Lemon
Lemon juice
Lemon peel
Lentils
Lentils yellow
Lime
Lychee
Lychee in Preserved
Mallow (Malva sylvestris) blossom tea
Mango
Maple syrup
Margarine
Margarine (diet)
Millet
Millet flakes
Miso paste (soy bean paste)
Mold cheese
Mozzarella
Mulberry fruit
Mullet
Mung bean
Mung bean sprouting
Mussels
Mutton
Olive oil
Orange
Orange juice
Oysters
Parmesan
Parsnip
Pear
Pear juice
Perch
Pimento
Pineapple
Pineapple (from a can)
Pineapple juice without sugar
Plaice
Plum
Pork meat
Pork skin
Quince
Radicchio
Radish
Radish (white, green, purple-red)
Raspberry

Raspberry dried (immature)
Reishi mushroom
Rhubarb
Romaine lettuce / lettuce salad
Sage
Salmon
Salsify
Sauerkraut (cutted cabbage fermented)
Seacrab
Sesame oil
Shark
Sorrel
Sour cherries
Sour cream 15% fat
Sour milk
Soy sauce
Soybean milk
Spelled (Dark) bread
Spelled grain
Spelled semolina
Spelled wholemeal flour
Spinach
Strawberries
Strawberry Juice
Sugar brown
Sugar candy white
Sugar cane sugar
Sugar fructose - fruit sugar

Sugar glucose - grapes sugar
Sugar Milk Sugar
Sugar white
Sunflower oil
Tangerine
Tarragon (Estragon)
Tomato
Trout
Tuna
Turkey breast meat
Vegetable juice
Wakame
Watermelon
Wheat
Wheat beer
Wheat bran
Wheat bulgur
Wheat flakes
Wheat flour
Wheat germ oil
Wheat semolina
Wheat semolina for children
Yarrow tea
Yogi tea
Yogurt (natural, 1.5% fat)
Yogurt (natural, 3.5% fat)
Zucchini

11 Complementary

11.1 Angelica (root)

Radix Angelica
preparation: Decoction
Expels wind, eliminates moisture, relieves the internal heat.
Decoction from 3-6 g, drink in two doses on an empty stomach.

11.2 Chili pods

Capsicum annuum, fruct.
preparation: Embrocation
Eliminates wind-cold. Warms up inner / Li, moves Heart-Qi and Blood.
High doses may lead to life-threatening hypothermia, prolonged use,
acute gastritis, inflammation of the kidneys. Capsicum preparations
irritate the skin and mucous membranes even in small quantities and may
cause painful burning sensations.

11.3 Cinnamon bark

Cinnamomum verum, cort.
preparation: Decoction
Warms channels, promotes yang and channel flow, reduces cold evil,
tonifies yang energy and warms.
Decoction from 2-5 g, drink in two doses on an empty stomach; to
increase the effect, add 2 g licorice root and 3 slices of ginseng.
Special features: In TCM, cinnamon is a very good supplement for many
other herbs, especially for yang tonic. It enhances the warming and
toning properties of herbal tinctures and improves their taste. Cinnamon
is one of the most warming remedies in Chinese herbal medicine, it
warms cold extremities and also internal organs
Do not use together with: onions and kaolin.

11.4 Coriander

Coriandri, Fructus
preparation: Different effects
Reduces inner wind. Tonifies and regulates stomach-qi. Directs wet heat
and wetness cold out of the bladder. Eliminates wind-cold. Regulates and
moves liver-qi.
Active ingredients: tannins, essential oil, vitamin C, sitosterol, protein
If measles or chickenpox have already broken out, do not use. Do not
overdose.

11.5 Ginger fresh

Zingiberis officinalis, Rhizoma
preparation: Decoction
Strengthens juices production, reduces cold-nuisance, stimulates,
stimulates the Yang-energy, warms the lung- and stomach-energy.
Put 1-6 slices of fresh root in a jug of water for 3 minutes. Drink 10 g in
two doses on empty stomach.
To improve the taste is brown raw sugar
Special features: In TCM, the fresh ginger root is mainly used against fish
poisoning and colds of the lungs and stomach.
Because ginger promotes nutrient uptake, it is often used in a variety of
formulations to facilitate the rapid absorption of other herbs and thereby
enhance their effects. Ginger contains the digestive enzyme zingibain.
The digestive effect of this substance is stronger than that of the enzyme
papain.
In too large quantities, ginger leads to constipation, Not to use in:
pregnancy, high fever.

11.6 Juniper berries

Juniperus, fruct.
preparation: Decoction
Dries out, heads down, activates Wei Qi. Relieves wind moisture and transforms. Tonifies Spleen-Qi, Stomach-Qi, Heart-Qi, Kidney-Qi and Kidney-Yang, warms the inside. Guides moisture and heat out of the bladder.
Pour 2 teaspoons of the tea into 250 ml of boiling water and leave for 10 minutes. Then sieve. Drink 2 to 3 cups per day as needed.
Avoid overdose, pregnant women and acute kidney patients should do without. External rubbing may cause blistering of the skin.

11.7 Lovage root

Levisticum officinale, rad.
preparation: Different effects
Dissolves moisture-cold and dissipates it. Regulates qi, moves and strengthens. Transforms moisture and mucus, warms inside. Eliminates wind-cold. Promotes wound healing.

11.8 Marjoram

Origanum majorana
preparation: Healing tea (infusion)
Scatters wind-cold of the surface. Emanating moisture and cold-mucus of the lungs, warms spleen- and stomach-yang.
Active ingredients: eth. Oil, bitter substances, tannins
Concomitant symptoms such as headache and dizziness with overdose are to be expected.

11.9 Sage

Salvia
preparation: Healing tea (infusion)
Expels Mucus, Dries, Guides Down, Activates Wei Qi, Strengthens Qi.
Äth. Oils containing many bitter substances and tannins should not be overdosed in order not to pollute the stomach.
Do not use on: Pregnancy

11.10 Sorrel

Rumex crispus, rad. / Rumex acetosa herb.
preparation: Different effects
Eliminates moisture-heat, dissipates heat-toxins, regulates liver-qi and intestinal-qi, dissipates wind-cold and heat-wetness.
Pour fresh or dried leaves with water and leave to soak for at least ten minutes.
Do not use during pregnancy and lactation.

12 Basics of Nutrition

The basic principles of nutrition described herein are general recommendations. They are not aimed at a specific form of therapy. Recommendations concerning a therapy have priority.

12.1 Nutrition

Regular meals in a relaxed atmosphere. A warm breakfast is considered a good start into the day.
The main meals ought to be taken for lunch – supper in the early evening. Pay attention to feeling hungry or sated: don't eat too much nor remain hungry is the rule
Prepare the meals freshly from natural, regional products. Frozen, heat-conserved, industrially prepared or foodstuffs cooked in the microwave oven are rejected.
Choice of foodstuffs according to the season: more cooling food in summer, more warming food in winter.
Eat cooked food at least twice a day. Food and drinks ought to be lukewarm, never ice-cold or hot.
Raw vegetables, briefly cooked vegetables, freshly squeezed juices and mineral water are not recommended. Milk and dairy products are only included in the diet if they don't cause problems. Don't use therapeutic recipes over a longer period without consulting your doctor or therapist.

Varied food
Enjoy the diversity of foodstuffs. Characteristics of a balanced nutrition are variety, suitable combination and a balanced quantity of rich and low energy foodstuffs (on one hand avoiding undersupply with essential nutrients and on the other hand to take to many undesirable substances).

A lot of Cereal Products - and Potatoes
Bread, pasta, rice, cereal flakes (best wholemeal) as well as potatoes

contain almost no fat, but many vitamins, mineral nutrients, trace elements, roughage and secondary plant substances. These foodstuffs ought to be taken with low-fat side dishes.

Vegetables and Fruit – „Take Five" every day … 5 portions of vegetables and fruit a day, as fresh as possible, briefly cooked, or maybe one portion as a juice – ideal as a side dish to every meal as well as snack between meals: Thus a lot of vitamins, mineral nutrients as well as roughage and secondary plant substances

Daily milk and dairy products
Milk and Dairy Products every Day, once or twice per Week Fish; meat, sausages as well as eggs moderately. These foodstuffs contain valuable nutrients like calcium in the milk, iodine selenium and omega-3 fat acids in saltwater fish. Meat is favorable due to its high content of disposable iron and the vitamins B1, B6 and B12. Quantities of 300 – 600 g meat and sausage per week are sufficient. Prefer low-fat products, especially in meat- and dairy products.

Low-fat and fatty Foodstuffs
Fat supplies us with essential fat acids and fatty foodstuffs contain also fat-soluble vitamins. Fat is high in energy; therefore much fat in the food may cause overweight, possibly also cancer. Too many saturated fat acids may further a tendency for cardic-vascular diseases in the long term. Prefer vegetable oils and fats (e.g. rapeseed-, olive-, soya-oils and solid fats produced therefrom). Beware of invisible fat in meat- and dairy products, pastry and sweets as well as in fast-food and convenience foods. 70 – 90 g fat per day is sufficient.

Moderately Sugar and Salt
Take sugar and foods/drinks containing various kinds of sugar (e.g. glucose syrup) only occasionally. Use herbs and spices as well as a little salt creatively. Prefer salt containing iodine.

Plenty of Liquids
Water is absolutely essential. Drink 1-2 l liquids every day. Prefer water (with or without gas) and other low-calorie drinks. Alcoholic drinks should not be taken.

Tasty Dishes, carefully cooked
Cook the meals with as low temperatures and as short as possible, using little water and fat – this preserves the original taste, keeps the nutrients intact and prevents the production of harmful compounds.

Take time and enjoy the food
Take your Time and enjoy your Food
Eating consciously helps to eat right. The eye enjoys food, too. It's fun, invites to enjoy varied dishes and stimulates the feeling of satiety.

Watch your Weight and stay in Motion
A balanced diet and a lot of exercise and sport (30 – 60 min/day) are a healthy combination. The right weight furthers well-being and health.
Thermals, directional effectiveness, digestive power
There are various criteria for judging the effectiveness of herbs and foodstuffs.
The use of certain herbs and ingredients is based on observations of the effects on the body which these foodstuffs, herbs and spices show after having eaten them. The medical science has developed following system: Every ingredient or herb has a directional effectiveness. Furthermore, there are herbs which have a special effect on certain organs.
The basic condition for a healthy metabolism is to obtain sufficient energy from food and that the digestive process doesn't use too much energy.
An easily digestible meal makes content and sated, doesn't cause flatulence and fatigue after the meal. The perfect spices increase the healthiness of our meals. Very often, just small doses of herbs and spices will suffice. They are not used to make us sated, but to help our digestive organs to digest the food.

12.2 Recipes

The recipes list the ingredients to be used and the cooking instructions show how the dish is prepared. The list of ingredients shows the concerned quantities as well as the relevance for the therapy. If you find „omit", try to comply or find an alternative from the „list of recommended foodstuffs". Mostly it shall result just in a small change of taste when you simply avoid this ingredient.
Mild cooking methods: boiling, stewing, poaching, steaming
Strong cooking methods: barbecuing, roasting, frying, smoking
Balanced cooking methods: deep-frying, baking brick
Deep-freezing and warming in the microwave oven should be avoided (denaturalization).

12.3 Foodstuffs

Foodstuffs have an effect on body and soul like medicinal herbs, only a very much milder one. Dietary advice is mainly based on regional

foodstuffs. The knowledge about the effects of each foodstuff and the knowledge, when which foodstuff shall be used, is based on the school medicine. Use ecologic-organic products, if possible. As everything should be cooked for a long time due to a better digestability and very rarely eaten raw, the food agrees with everyone.
The classification of the foodstuffs according to their effect on the body is the basis in order to achieve a harmonious status of health.
Dietary advisors do not recommend certain foodstuffs for everyone. The individual diet is tailor-made for the individual constitution.

Buy only fresh and ripe fruit and vegetables. You ought to leave unripe fruit and vegetables and such with brown spots and wilted leaves behind in the market. In this case take deep-frozen goods (never ready-to-serve dishes!). Fruit and vegetables are deep-frozen immediately after harvesting and often contain more vitamins and minerals than the goods from the vegetable shelf. Whereas conserved or tinned goods contain very much less biological substances. Also, salt, sugar and others are mostly added to the latter. Never leave the foodstuffs in the water after washing them to avoid that many vital substances get drowned. Clean salads, fruit and vegetables immediately before serving.

Please make sure of the hygienic processing of foodstuffs. Clean your salads, fruit and vegetables carefully. When cooking with meat, prepare all ingredients first and then process the meat products. Clean the worktop and tools very carefully. Wooden surfaces ought to be treated with a mild disinfectant regularly in order to reduce germination.
Store fruit and vegetables separately, if possible. Harvested fruit and vegetables are still alive and emit e.g. ethylene gas, which makes other products ripen and age faster. Keep meat and fish in the closed packaging or store them in the fridge in closed containers.

12.4 Herbs

There are some basic rules for storing medicinal herbs. On principle, herbs must be protected from direct sunlight, humidity and heat.

Containers for the storage of herbs may be glasses, ceramic jars and even plastic containers. However, plastic is a rather unsuitable material and should only be a short-term solution. In case of glass containers, use a dark material.

Medicinal herbs cannot be kept for any long period. The shelf life of herbs is limited. However, it can be prolonged with suitable storage. The place should be dark, rather cool and absolutely dry. A wooden medicine cabinet, placed not directly next to a source of heat, would be ideal. Never buy large quantities of herbs so as not to have to throw them away. Label the container with the name of the herb and the date of harvesting or processing.

13 Other dietic-books

The following syndromes of dietetics, TCM or for a therapy supplement for cancer are available.

Dietetics

E001. Nutrition of the infant - baby food
E002. Nutrition during lactation
E003. Nutrition in old age
E004. Nutrition of children and adolescents
E005. Nutrition of athletes
E006. Light weight
E007. Pregnancy
E008. Full food

Protein and electrolyte - kidneys
E009. (hemodialysis) dialysis treatment
E010. Acute renal failure
E011. Chronic renal insufficiency
E012. Nephrotic syndrome
E013. Kidney stones (nephrolithiasis)

Gastrointestinal tract - pancreas
E014. Acute pancreatitis (inflammation of the pancreas)
E015. Chronic pancreatitis (inflammation of the pancreas)

Gastrointestinal tract - small intestine and large intestine
E016. Acute obstipation (constipation)
E017. Chronic obstipation (constipation)
E018. Colon irritabile
E019. Diverticulitis
E020. Acquired lactose intolerance (lactose malabsorption)
E021. Fructose malabsorption
E022. Glutensensitive enteropathy (celiac disease)
E023. Colectomy
E024. Short Bowel Syndrome

Gastrointestinal tract - liver, gallbladder, bile ducts
E025. Acute and chronic hepatitis (inflammation of the liver)
E026. Cholelithiasis (bile stones)
E027. fatty liver

E028. cirrhosis

Gastrointestinal tract - Stomach and duodenal intestine
E029. Acute gastritis
E030. Chronic gastritis
E031. Stomach bleeding
E032. Ulcus ventriculi and duodenal ulcer
E033. Condition after gastric surgery

Gastrointestinal tract - oral cavity and esophagus
E034. Stomatitis
E035. Esophageal carcinoma (esophageal cancer)
E036. Refluosophagitis (heartburn)

Special diseases
E037. Phenylketonuria (PKU)
E038. Rheumatic joint diseases

Metabolism
E039. Obesity (overweight)
E040. Diabetes mellitus
E041. Eating disorders (underweight)

Fat metabolism
E042. Hypercholesterolaemia (increased cholesterol level)
E043. Hepatic Encephalopathy

Heart and circulation
E044. Arteriosclerosis (arterial calcification)
E045. Heart insufficiency
E046. Hypertension
E047. Hyperuricaemia and gout

Changed nutrient requirements
E048. In case of fever
E049. For malignant diseases
E050. After burns
E051. Radiation and chemotherapy

CANCER
E100. Pancreatic cancer
E101. Bladder cancer
E102. Blood cancer (leukemia)
E103. Breast cancer
E104. Colorectal cancer
E105. Gastric cancer
E106. Kidney cancer
E107. Esophageal cancer

TCM
E200. Bladder - moisture heat in the bladder
E201. Bladder - moisture and cold in the bladder

E202. Bladder - emptiness and cold in the bladder
E203. Large intestine - external cold affects the large intestine
E204. Large intestine - moisture heat in the large intestine
E205. Large intestine - heat blocks the intestine II acute
E206. Large intestine - dryness of the colon
E207. Large intestine - Yang deficiency (cold)
E208. Heart - Blood insufficiency
E209. Heart - Blood stagnation
E210. Heart - Fire
E211. Heart - Hot mucus clogs the heart pores
E212. Heart - Cold mucus clogs the heart pores
E213. Heart - Qi deficiency
E214. Heart - Yang deficiency
E215. Heart - Yin deficiency
E216. Liver - Ascending Liver Yang
E217. Liver - Blood deficiency
E218. Liver - Blood stagnation
E219. Liver - Moisture heat in liver and gall bladder
E220. Liver - Fire
E221. Liver - Gall bladder Qi-Empty
E222. Liver - Cold in the liver meridian
E223. Liver - Qi stagnation
E224. Liver - Wind
E225. Liver - Wind with ascending liver Yang
E226. Liver - Wind with blood anemic
E227. Liver - Wind with extreme heat
E228. Lung - Qi deficiency
E229. Lung - Mucus-moisture in the lungs
E230. Lung - Mucus-heat in the lungs
E231. Lung - Mucus-cold in the lungs
E232. Lung - Dryness of the lungs
E233. Lung - Wind-heat attacks the lungs
E234. Lung - Wind-cold affects the lungs
E235. Lung - Yin deficiency
E236. Stomach - Bloodstagnation
E237. Stomach - Fire
E238. Stomach - Cold with liquid
E239. Stomach - Nutrition stagnation
E240. Stomach - Qi deficiency
E241. Stomach - Rebellious Qi
E242. Stomach - Yin Emptiness
E243. Spleen - Heat and moisture attack the spleen
E244. Spleen - Coldness and moisture affects the spleen
E245. Spleen - Qi deficiency
E246. Spleen - Qi deficiency + Declining spleen Qi
E247. Spleen - Qi deficiency + spleen does not control the blood
E248. Spleen - Yang deficiency
E249. Kidney - Heart and kidney no longer communicate
E250. Kidney - Jing deficiency
E251. Kidney - Kidneys cannot receive the Qi
E252. Kidney - Qi is not stable
E253. Kidney - Yang deficiency
E254. Kidney - Yin deficiency

For further information visit nutribook.info.

14 EBNS - Software for nutritional counseling

The main task of the database is to create personalized nutritional advice for each patient individually. The database was developed for Dietetics and Traditional Chinese Medicine.
The Database supports training and advices in the daily work routine.

The computer program provides lists of recipes, ingredients and herbs, which are given to the client. individually adjustable according to patient's request from whole food to vegetarians (lacto, ovo, ...). For every register there is an information sheet which can be given to the client. All texts can be individually designed.

The syndromes can be combined and result in an intersection of the recommended recipes and ingredients. The automated diagnosis for the TCM enables you to check your experience during the training as well as to confirm your diagnosis in the working day. You select several predefined symptoms and have the program automatically display the relevant syndromes.

How to work with the database:
Select the patient / client, select one or more of the syndromes you diagnosed and print the folder.

You can change all values, create new symptoms or syndromes, develop recipes, change or adapt ingredients and herbs to your findings. In simple client management, all relevant data about the person is stored. You get an overview of the past diagnoses and the development of the course of the disease.

As a consultant you save a lot of time when you print out the recipe, food and herbal lists for the recognized syndromes and give them to the clients. You can use this time for a personal conversation. With the database, dieticians and nutritionists can view the nutrients and trace elements for each recipe and develop recipes for syndromes even with suggested ingredients.

All recipe and grocery lists can also be ordered from me as a combination of several diseases. I wish all readers good luck, health and happiness in life.
More information can be found at www.ebns.at.
Volunteer: www.krebsinfo.at
Josef Miligui

.